Thrift Store Reselling Secrets You Wish You Knew

50 Different Items You Can Buy At Thrift Stores And Sell On eBay And Amazon For Huge Profit

Table of Contents

Introduction

I want to thank you and congratulate you for downloading the book, Thrift Store Reselling Secrets You Wish You Knew.

This book contains proven steps and strategies on how to know what you should look for in the thrift stores and flip for big money on eBay and Amazon.

If you are looking into purchasing items from thrift stores and reselling them on Amazon or eBay, you need all of the information in this book. In this book you are going to find all of the top items that you need to keep your eye out for when you are thrift shopping. These items are going to bring in a large profit for you and most of them are not difficult to find.

You are also going to be given tips about how to make your listings work for you and how you can make sure you earn a profit from all of the items you are listing. Finally, you are going to learn what mistakes you don't want to do while you are learning to flip thrift store items.

Thanks again for downloading this book, I hope you enjoy it!

Chapter 1
The Right Strategy to Get Started Reselling

Before I start teaching you about all of the things you can purchase at a thrift store and sell on Amazon or eBay for a profit, I want share with you some important information. You shouldn't plan on just going to the thrift shop, grabbing a few items, listing them and making a profit. If you are going to make money selling the items you find at a thrift store on Amazon or Ebay, you need to first know what you are looking for! I am going to help you with that. Second, you need to understand that most people who do this work at it full time, often spending more than 40 hours a week on it.

The next thing that you need to know is that often times you can go digging through all of the stuff at thrift stores, spending your entire day searching and come home with nothing. So it can be difficult at times. It all depends on being at the right place at the right time.

You also need to weed out the pointless thrift shops, the ones that price things so high you will not be able to make a profit. For example, I found a leather jacket in good condition last week. The store wanted $50 for it but the most I could sell this for would be $60 and chances are I wouldn't even make that much. Small profits are not going to keep you going if you really want to get into this business. On the other hand, if you watch for sales at these stores you will be able to get much bigger profits. You see, the next day that same leather jacket was on sale for $25. This gave me a much better chance at making a profit. It was sold on eBay for $58.43.

So don't go into a thrift shop determined to find something. You have to be patient and if someone purchases your items before they go on sale, don't sweat it.

For the first item, I want to talk about brand names. You would expect that all known name brands would sell great, but that is not the case.

1. Item number one is Diesel Viker Mens jeans. You can sell these for a fairly good profit on eBay as well as Amazon if you can find them. One such sale was finding them for $6 at the thrift store and selling them for a little over $60. You do need to make sure they are in good condition and have all of the buttons and zippers. Always remember when inspecting clothing in the thrift store, try and find an area with good lighting so you can clearly inspect the piece of clothing you are thinking about buying.

2. Video games. There are tons of gaming systems, but what you want to look for is the older video games. Stuff like Super Mario Bros for Nintendo or Waterworld for Atari 2600. Game boy games sell great too. Rare games can often sell for $150 and can be purchased for about a buck at thrift stores. It is important that you look at the packaging because a game that would sell for $200 in good packaging will only sell for about $50 in torn packaging. Of course if it has never been opened it is worth more! In addition, always be on the lookout for prototype games for any system. These are games that are often extremely rare as they are in an unfinished state yet sometimes they slip through the cracks and end up in the thrift stores. These types of games can bring in huge amounts of profit!

3. As far as shirts go you want to focus on Polo shirts in the big and tall sizes. Remember that in general, the crazier and louder the design, the higher dollar amount it will usually sell for. These will sell quickly and you will be able to make a good profit on them. Most thrift stores will sell them for around $2 each and you can easily sell them for $20. In addition, always be on the lookout for vintage mens hawaiian shirts. If you see a

vintage hawaiian shirt from the late 50's through early 70's, be sure to do some research on it by looking at the completed listings on eBay. Some of these early hawaiian shirts can bring in massive money. In general, the more vibrant the design, the more money you can count on coming your way in profits!

4. Shoes are an item that many people overlook, but it is something you really need to consider looking at to resell. If you can find Adidas, Nike or Trek shoes, you can usually purchase them for a couple of bucks and make about $50 - $75 per pair. You need to make sure they are in good condition, check the tread and the inside of the shoe. The older the shoe is, the more you can make off of it. Watch for shoes from the 70's and 80's. Keep an eye out for vintage Vans and Converse shoes.

5. Cassette tapes, VHS tapes, Disney movies still in the original packaging. Let's start with the cassette tapes and VHS tapes. These can be any brand and need to be blank and in the original packaging. In fact, any obsolete media can be sold on eBay and Amazon for a profit as long as they have not been used and are in the original packaging! These are very easy to find and you can purchase them fairly cheap usually a few bucks for a set. Disney movies on VHS tape are also a great way to make money. Anything that was made in the 90's or earlier will sell usually sell quickly. If you find a thrift shop that has VHS tapes in their original box, you have found a gold mine. The great thing about these tapes is that they are easy to ship and don't take up a lot of space. You can also purchase them for about a 50 cents. Peter Pan is selling for about $3 while Davy Crockett is selling for about $15. This is a great return on your investment and can be a quick flip.

Chapter 2
Get a Smart Phone and Start Making Money

No matter how many items I list in this book, there are always going to be items in the thrift shops that you will come across and not know if they have any value. Even if you don't think the item has value, you still need to go ahead and use your cell phone to look it up on either eBay or Amazon. If you find that you can make at least 3x the investment price on either site you need to pick it up.

For example there was a flour mill at one of the thrift shops I frequently go to, it was priced at $20. To me that is a little high for a thrift shop, but I decided to look it up and found I could list it for $250 and turn it into a profit quickly. Of course I bought it but had I not had my smart phone I would have passed it by.

6. Toys!!! There are so many different toys that you can find that can earn you a ton of money. To start off we are going to talk about toy guns. This is a place where you can earn a great return, but you need to understand some thrift stores know what they have and won't sell them cheaply. One of the toy guns that is going for about $100 right now is a 1960's Lone Ranger Winchester rifle cap gun. If you find any toy guns from the 60's you are going to be able to make this kind of money, but watch for Winchester replicas. The price of this gun at a thrift shop is about $10 giving you a $90 profit.

7. Marx figurines are also something you need to keep your eye out for. It does not matter if they are plastic or metal. These sell quickly and you can make a great

profit on them. One plastic figurine can be purchased for less than a $1 and easily sold for $10. A Popeye figurine is worth over a thousand dollars!

8. Vintage bobble head dolls are another thing you need to be on the lookout for. A set of Beetles bobble head dolls can go for as much as $5,000 and only cost about $100 at a thrift store. Any bobble head from the 60's that is in good condition can bring you a ton of money.

9. Vintage Lincoln Logs turn up in thrift stores all the time. The great thing about these is that you don't have to have a set or a box even, a simple mixed lot of Lincoln Logs can bring in $150 easily.

10. Books are not going to get you a ton of money unless you can find vintage Betty Crocker cookbooks. The older the better and they need to be in good to mint condition. Make sure all of the pages are there and they are not written on or stained.

11. Another book you need to watch out for is old Disney coloring books. They usually sell for about a quarter and you can sell them for up to $10. You need to make sure that again, all of the pages are there and they have not been scribbled on. Some will still sell if they have a few pages colored but I try to avoid these all together.

12. College books are another great item to keep an eye out for. If you live near a college town make sure to check out the thrift stores there. When purchasing college books, don't pay more than a few dollars and make sure they have any computer disks needed with them. You can easily get $20 -$30 for these books on Amazon or Ebay.

13. Tupperware is the next item I want to discuss. You need to make sure that it is real Tupperware and is in good

condition. Wash it well before you take a photo of it to post and list any stains or issues with the Tupperware.

14. Anything Peanuts. All things Charlie Brown sell quickly and for a good price. Recently I saw a Peanuts doll sell for over a grand on eBay. Even the Peanuts sheet sets sell quickly.

15. Another toy to watch out for is Hulk Smash Hands. I consistently see these at thrift stores for $1 per set and they are selling for between $15 and $25 per set on eBay.

Chapter 3
Always Have a Plan B

If you purchase an item and it doesn't sell, what are you going to do with it? Do you have an area to store items while they sit on your store shelf or do you want to hold a garage sale and try to get rid of them that way? One thing that you don't want to do is donate them back to the store you bought them from. Even if you paid a quarter for it, do whatever you can to at least earn that quarter back. Allowing yourself to lose money no matter how small is not a habit you want to get into.

16. Hand held games are the next item. There are games like Yahtzee, Bridge and Nintendo Crystal Balloon Fight that sell anywhere between $40 and $300 depending on the rarity of the game. These were very popular in the 90's and even though they can be hard to find, they are worth the few bucks you will pay for them. Always be on the lookout for vintage Nintendo game and watch handheld systems. These were popular in the early 80's and always fetch a pretty penny on eBay.

17. Old electronics sell for just a few dollars at thrift stores and if you find brands like Sony or Panasonic, you can make quite a bit of money off of them. You need to make sure they are in fairly good condition and ensure they have all of the cords with them. If they do not have the cords find out how much it is going to cost to get replacement cords before purchasing the item.

18. Children's clothes sell great as well but you need to watch for brand names. Gymboree and Hanna Anderson are some of the best selling brands of children's clothing and of course you need to make sure it is not stained or snagged. You also shouldn't pay more than $3 for these items if you want to make any type of profit.

19. Raggedy Ann and Andy dolls are an item I see a lot of at thrift stores but even though you can sell these for up to $100, you need to be very careful and only purchase the originals. Spending $30 on a set of 1990 Raggedy Anne and Andy dolls is not going to get you any money, as a matter of fact that is about all they are worth.

20. Large plush toys sell for upwards of $100 as well. You want to watch for plush toys such as Wily Coyote or Scooby Doo. The bigger they are, the more money they will go for. This is one item many people overlook.

21. Any World War 2 toys will pull in a huge profit as well. Always make sure they are authentic and in good condition before purchasing.

22. Pokémon! Anything Pokémon will sell. There are Pikachu plush toys, key chains and even Nintendo games. If you can find Pokémon items still in their package, you are going to be able to make a lot of money. Many of the Nintendo DS Pokémon games still have a high resale value.

23. I want to end this chapter by talking about Star Wars items and Barbie Dolls. If the Star Wars items are still in their original package you should invest in them. If they are not, go ahead and pass them up because you will not see much profit, unless the Stars Wars toys are early 80's and authentic. Barbie is something that so many people think is going to make them a lot of money, but unless you find the original Barbie in her box, you are not going to make much of a profit. eBay and Amazon are saturated with Barbie sellers, so right now it is best to avoid them.

Chapter 4
Look For the Odd and Unusual

You need to watch for things that are not often found when it comes to thrift shopping. You need to look for anything that is odd or rare. When I saw a 1911 cathedral radio at a thrift store, it did not catch my eye because I knew what I was looking at. Instead it caught my eye because it was odd and I had never seen it before. You can purchase items like a bread maker at thrift stores all day long. This means they have very little resale value. However, finding something that you don't normally see like a 1911 radio is where you will make the most money.

24. That brings us to radios. You don't want to purchase just any radio when you are shopping. Keep your eye out for Philco radios. These are old antique radios that contain tubes. I purchased one for $25 because I liked the way it looked. I was going to keep it for myself until I found out I could sell it for $450.

25. Original Nintendo Systems will sell for a ton of money as well. The more games you can sell with the system the more money you will get. You also want to watch for extra remote controllers as well as the gun for Duck Hunt. If you ever see original NES Nintendo games sealed, always pick them up. You can make a ton of money selling sealed vintage games. When researching NES Nintendo games, always check the completed listings on eBay. If you find a game in the thrift shop and you are unsure of its resale value, take a quick look at the completed listings on eBay. This will give you all the information you need to decide whether or not it will be a profitable item for you. Remember, if the game comes with the original box and instructions, that is a sure sign that you have struck gold. Any NES Nintendo

game that you can find complete, should bring in a very nice profit. Especially if you can get these games under $5.

26. Vintage posters also sell very well. If you can find Sonic the Hedgehog posters or a New Kids on the Block poster from the eighties you can sell them pretty quickly for about $10. I have regularly found music posters from 1980's new wave bands that have sold upwards of $50. Keep your eye out music posters from obscure bands from the 1980's.

27. Sony handheld camcorders are a great find. I have found several of these at thrift stores for $5 and they go from $50-$75 dollars each. They sell for more if they come with the original case. Check to make sure all of the components are there and that it works. You should also check for an instruction manual which will bring in even more money.

28. Keep an eye out for old sports Jerseys. You can easily find a Michael Jordan Chicago Bulls basketball jersey and purchase it for $7 then list it for $60 and sell it quickly. Make sure it is in good condition and doesn't smell musty. If the clothes you are selling smell musty and moldy, people will expect a refund. If you do find a great item that smells bad, simply washing it and using vinegar in the washing machine can work wonders. Always pay attention to the washing instructions on the care tag before washing.

29. Art is great to buy at thrift stores as well, if they get a lot of estate donations. If you are going to purchase art you need to know what you are looking for. For example you can find a Picasso print for $30 at a resale shop and list it for a good profit, but if you don't know it is a Picasso print you could just pass it up.

30. To finish up this chapter I want to talk about one more item that many people overlook, coffee mugs. Certain coffee mugs are very collectable and you can sell them for $5-$25 dollars each depending on the brand. What you want to watch for is anything Disney and Starbucks. Also, coffee mugs with a very unique theme also do quite well and can net a nice profit.

Chapter 5
Expand Your Horizons

Don't just limit yourself to purchasing items at thrift stores. Try going to some estate sales and even flea markets. Another great way to make money is watch for clearance items at your local stores. End of season sales and after holiday sales will give you great deals if you don't mind holding on to items until next year. This is one reason why storage is so important when it comes to selling on eBay and Amazon.

31. Silver. I don't have a specific name brand for you here but trust me, you can find silver at thrift stores. It is often put on the shelf by mistake with the rest of the utensils so you need to know how to spot it! Now you may be thinking that no one is going to buy a spoon here or a fork here, but this is what they know that you need to know. Silver no matter what form it takes is still silver and people will buy this stuff!

32. Comic books can have great resale value. Especially old Marvel comic books that are in good condition. You need to make sure they are not damaged, that the pages are all there and if you can find them in mint condition you are going to make even more. You can sell comic books all day long online, so anytime you have the chance to pick them up do it.

33. Watch out for 80's GI Joes. Many of these can go for a couple hundred dollars. Even GI Joe parts sell for a lot more than you would expect, so keep your eyes out for them. Make sure they are real GI Joes and not something you would purchase from a dollar store.

34. Winter coats can also bring in some good money if you are willing to hold on to them if they do not sell

immediately. You can easily find vintage Pendleton coats for $2 or $3 each and sell them for close to $100 during the winter time. If you find them at the end of the season you can get them and hold on to them until the next season. Always be on the lookout for Patagonia, North Face and Spyder jackets.

35. Remington adding machines. Up until this point we have talked mostly about items that are fairly light and not too difficult to ship, but an adding machine is much heavier. This weight and extra shipping costs do not seem to bother the buyers, in fact you can purchase one of these for $3-$5 at a thrift store and list it for $30 without a problem.

36. This one does not have a brand name but you should really keep an eye out for beads and jewelry making supplies. Many people are taking up jewelry making and beads are expensive! I found several strings of beads for a quarter a piece, took them off the string bagged them up and sold them for $5 each. Easy money and easy to ship.

37. Blood pressure machines sell regularly for $35 to $40 so if you can purchase one for $4 or $5 you can easily sell it for $20 on eBay or Amazon. One thing I like to do is carry a few AA batteries with me so that when I find these items, I can make sure they work before I spend my money on them.

38. Care Bears are an item that I love picking up. They have to be the original Care Bears from the 80's and you can usually get them for $1 each. They easily go for $20 to avid collectors.

39. Previously I said you should avoid most clothes, but if you can find concert T-shirts pick them up. These again need to be from the 80's or earlier and you need to make sure it is not a replica, but once you do this you

can earn some quick cash. You can usually pick up a T-shirt for $2 and sell them for as high as $75 depending on what concert tour it was from. An Aerosmith T-shirt can get you $50 while a Led Zeppelin can go for $125. There is huge money to be made selling vintage concert shirts. It is more difficult to find these shirts in the thrift shops these days. However, you can still find these treasures on the racks!

40. The last thing I want to talk to you about in this chapter is fur. There is no brand name for this one, as long as it is real fur and it is cheap buy it. I want to make it clear that if the store knows what they have, they will mark the price up. I went to a resale shop that advertised they had received a lot of new fur coats in, they priced them at over $500 each. On the other hand if you are just going through a store and find a fur coat for a few dollars, do not pass it up. Check to make sure it is real fur. This will be marked on the tag and you can often smell them to make sure it is real. This next tip is very important. Check the lining and make sure that if it is loose, you can have it fixed fairly cheap. Be ready for it to sell fast! Even though many people are protesting 'new' fur, they have no problem buying old fur and actually prefer it.

Chapter 6
Be Consistent and Stay Focused

Hopefully the advice that I have given you at the beginning of each of these chapters has helped you, but what I am going to tell you now could be the most important advice I could ever give you. List regularly and list often! If you do not list often you are going to see your listings dropping down and not getting seen by most people. The same thing is going to happen if you do not list regularly. This will cause you to see a drop in sales.

I am not saying you have to list 30 items a day, but if you go out and purchase 10 items don't list them all at once. List one each day and then plan a new trip to get more items. You will see your sales grow if you list regularly and often.

41. Harry Potter books. I did mention earlier that most books won't sell, but if you do see Harry Potter books you need to pick them up. Set them to the side and hold onto them watching out for more each time you shop. Once you have a complete set, list it and watch how much you can sell it for. If you want to get the most profit possible, I suggest not paying more than a couple of bucks per book, even better purchase on days when books are marked down to a quarter!

42. Figurines are always for sale at thrift shops, but you need to keep an eye out for Holly Hobby. Most of the figurines you will find are going to be worthless but Holly Hobby sells very well. Flip the figurine over and look for the Holly Hobby label on the bottom. Of course, just like with almost everything, you are going to be purchasing at thrift stores, you don't want to pay

more than a few bucks for each one and you want to make sure there are no cracks or chips in the figurines.

43. Another strange item you can make money with is JC Pennies and Sears catalogs. Many people will remember getting these each year at about Christmas time, and for some reason they want to purchase them today. Call it remembering their childhood if you must, but for whatever reason they are willing to pay up to $25 for a catalog you can find at a thrift store for about $2.

44. As you can see, there are many great items that sell and many odd items. I don't know whether to say this item is odd or cute, or really what to call it, but novelty ties are a huge seller. You can purchase these for about 50 cents each and sell them for up to $15. You should watch for ties with themes such as The Simpsons, McDonalds, Disney, and Garfield. Of course there are tons and tons more ties that will sell, remember look for the rare items.

45. Costumes for your pets is another item you should keep your eyes out for. You can get these very cheap during the Halloween season and sell them all year long. People love to dress up their pets and for some reason dog bridal gowns sell really well. These do not have to be any specific brand but you need to make sure they are in good condition and clean.

What is going to make you successful when it comes to buying from thrift shops and selling on eBay and Amazon? Timing. We have all heard it but timing really is everything. If you find an item that is selling quickly that you can make a good profit on, sell it now. Don't slack off and not list the item.

One story was of a seller who listed an RC airplane that he purchased for $25 at a thrift store. He sold it for over $300 and just six months later another seller couldn't get more than $50 for the one he had listed.

This happens all the time. What is hot today may not be hot tomorrow and you need to stay on top of your game!

List your items and if the prices drop, don't get rid of your items. Remove the listing and simply hold on to the item until the prices go up again.

Patience is key when it comes to selling on eBay and Amazon. Your first listing is going to seem like it is taking forever if you just sit there and watch it. I know a lady who posted her first listing and literally sat there watching each bid be put in. She was miserable. Then I also know of a guy who posted his listing, left it alone for two days and was amazed to see that he earned $150 dollars from it.

List the items and leave it alone. Don't sit there and torture yourself for hours at a time watching the bids come in.

You also need to consider the amount of money that eBay, Amazon and PayPal are going to charge you. Carefully examine all of the listing and closing fees for the eBay item category you are listing in. Also, make sure you are aware of the PayPal fees as well. This is why I told you that you should not mess with an item unless you are sure you are going to make at least 3-5 times the amount of money you have in it.

Chapter 7

Set Your Goals and Make a Plan

Too often I have seen people jump into thrift shop flipping and not have a plan or any goals which of course leads to failure. So set up your goals, but don't get all crazy about the amount of money you want to make. It is very possible to make $1,000 dollars a month flipping part time but you are not going to make this starting out.

I was talking to a friend who was very interested in getting into flipping, but when they tried they wanted to make $1,000 a month. The first month they listed their items and made over $400 but became disappointed because they did not reach their goals.

I was so amazed that they were disappointed because I saw it as a win, they on the other hand did not. I had to explain to them that they needed to allow themselves time to work up to the goal of $1,000 dollars per month. So make sure you start with an obtainable goal that will pay for the time you spend flipping.

Now to finish up with the final five items you need to watch for when thrift shopping.

46. Puff the Magic Dragon is such a favorite for so many people. I remember when I got mine when I was a kid and how much I loved him. Once I grew up and learned about Puff, I wished I had not lost him all of those years ago. Now think about how many other people are out there wishing they still had their Puff and looking for a new one. As a matter of fact you can find one of these for just a couple of bucks and sell them for $30 each.

47. Scrabble tiles are once again of the odd things that sell online and that you can get for next to nothing. I actually have a deal with several thrift stores, they save all of the loose Scrabble tiles they find for me and I keep

them from going in the garbage. Once a month I make my rounds and pick up tiles. Depending on how any you can collect, you can sell them for between $10 and $100 so it is important to get as many as you can.

48. Disney characters. We all know you can get money for selling Mickey and Minnie mouse items. However, you can also turn a good profit with Pluto, Donald Duck, even fining a Flounder toy from the movie The Little Mermaid can make you $15. You should watch for plush toys, posters, small plastic toys, anything that is Disney.

49. Remember the Walk Man CD players from the 90's? These are a great seller. I find these all the time at thrift stores for $4 or $5 each and they sell for between $25 and $50 each. You want to try and get the ones that are still in the packaging if you want to make the most money, but don't pass up the ones that are not still in the original packaging because you can still make money on them with no problems. Use those batteries I told you to carry around with you and test the Walk Man to make sure it works. It is also good to have a CD available to test out if possible, as well as a set of ear buds because not all Walk Men are going to come with these items. You want to make sure you are not wasting your money on broken items.

50. Portable typewriters, the typewriters that you don't have to plug in. These are one of my favorite items to purchase and resell. They can be purchased for about $5 each and sell at about $60 or more. I find these all of the time. I actually found 7 in one day!

There are so many items that you can purchase at a thrift store and resale for a profit on eBay and Amazon. There is no way I can go over every item in this book, but when you are out and you are shopping at thrift stores you need to remember what I have mentioned several times in this book. Look for the odd, the obscure and the rare. If you see something you have never seen before look it up on your smart phone! You can easily use eBay to judge what the value of the item you are looking at is.

There you have it 50 items that you can go out and look for in your local thrift stores right now, but don't limit yourself to just the local thrift stores. Make sure you look for a few in some upscale neighborhoods, this is where you are going to find the best items. Don't forget to look at estate sales, yard sales and even storage unit auctions. Look everywhere you can to find great used items for your listings.

But remember to take it slow. Don't start out spending 40 hours a week doing this and investing $500 a week. Start with about $30-$40 to invest, turn a profit and get your money out of it. After that you can work with the profit to earn more and more!

Conclusion

Thank you again for downloading this book!

I hope this book was able to help you to understand that there are tons of items you can purchase at thrift stores and flip on eBay and Amazon.

The next step is to decide how much you want to invest, set your goals and get to the nearest thrift store!

Finally, if you enjoyed this book, then I'd like to ask you for a favor, would you be kind enough to leave a review for this book on Amazon? It'd be greatly appreciated!

Click here to leave a review for this book on Amazon!

Thank you and good luck!

Check Out My Other Books

Below you'll find some of my other popular books that are popular on Amazon and Kindle as well. Simply click on the links below to check them out. Alternatively, you can visit my author page on Amazon to see other work done by me.

http://www.amazon.com/Turning-Thrift-Store-Finds-Into-ebook/dp/B00S33XFXK

http://www.amazon.com/eBay-Selling-Secrets-Massive-Profits-ebook/dp/B00TJMBJDM

http://www.amazon.com/Unlocking-Etsy-Goldmine-Profitable-Business-ebook/dp/B00P35V5I8

http://www.amazon.com/Ultimate-Instagram-Marketing-Guide-Successful-ebook/dp/B00QUCPGWE

http://www.amazon.com/Unlocking-eBay-Goldmine-Maintain-Profitable-ebook/dp/B00Q7O0Z1W

http://www.amazon.com/Passive-Income-Goldmine-Creative-Financial-ebook/dp/B00PGCU0LG